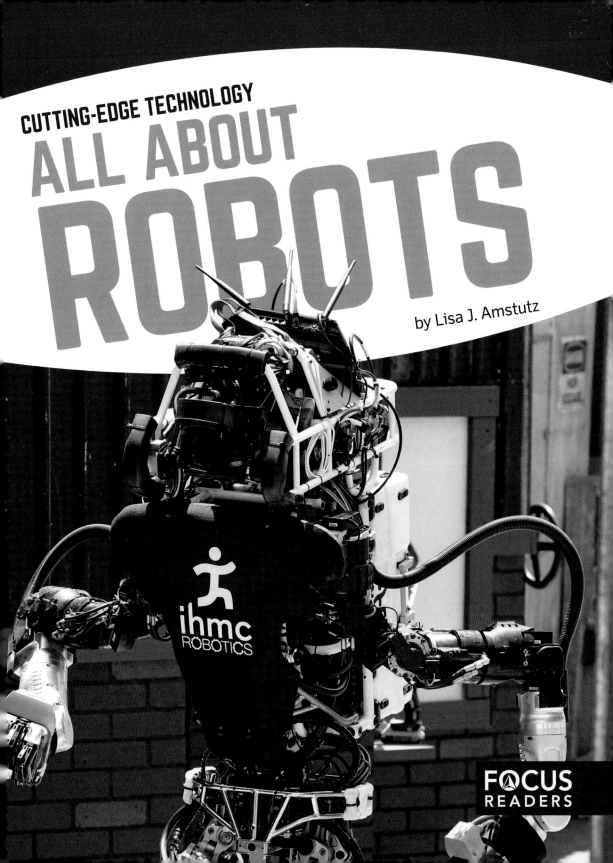

CUTTING-EDGE TECHNOLOGY

ALL ABOUT
ROBOTS

by Lisa J. Amstutz

ihmc ROBOTICS

FOCUS
READERS

North Star
EDITIONS

WWW.NORTHSTAREDITIONS.COM

Produced for North Star Editions by Red Line Editorial.

Photographs ©: Alex Gallardo/AP Images, cover, 1; NorGal/Shutterstock Images, 4–5; Lightspring/Shutterstock Images, 7; Featureflash Photo Agency/Shutterstock Images, 9; Nataliya Hora/Shutterstock Images, 10–11; bibiphoto/Shutterstock Images, 13; Navin Mistry/Shutterstock Images, 14–15; NASA, 17, 27; hans engbers/Shutterstock Images, 18–19; NASA/JPL-Caltech/Malin Space Science Systems, 21; Master Video/Shutterstock Images, 23; Peter Cihelka/The Free Lance-Star/AP Images, 24–25; Steve Lagreca/Shutterstock Images, 28–29

Content Consultant: Dr. Stelian Coros, Assistant Professor, Robotics Institute, Carnegie Mellon University

ISBN
978-1-63517-014-6 (hardcover)
978-1-63517-070-2 (paperback)
978-1-63517-175-4 (ebook pdf)
978-1-63517-125-9 (hosted ebook)

Library of Congress Control Number: 2016949755

Printed in the United States of America
Mankato, MN
November, 2016

ABOUT THE AUTHOR

Lisa J. Amstutz is the author of more than 50 nonfiction books for children. She specializes in topics related to science, nature, and agriculture. Lisa's work has also appeared in a variety of magazines and newspapers. Her background includes a BA in biology and an MS in environmental science.

TABLE OF CONTENTS

CHAPTER 1

WHAT IS A ROBOT?

Imagine waking up in the morning to find your breakfast already cooked and the table set by a robot. While you eat, robots do your laundry and vacuum the floor. Then you hop into your self-driving car and head to school. There, a robot teacher helps you with your math.

The first robotic vacuum cleaners became available in the 1990s.

Believe it or not, all of these robots already exist! Some of them are not yet widely available. But they will likely be more common in the future.

Robots are machines that are used to do tasks. The study of robots is called robotics. The scientists who make robots are called roboticists.

Robots come in many shapes and sizes. Most are made of metal and plastic. They have movable parts and follow commands. Some can sense things around them. Robots usually have at least one arm. Some robots are microscopic. Scientists are testing **nanobots** that are small enough to go inside the body.

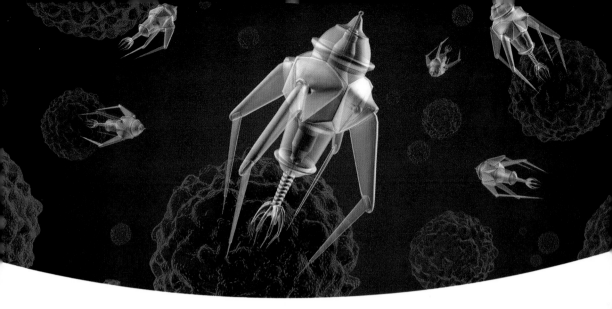

In the future, nanobots may be the size of cells.

These tiny robots can find problems and fix them.

People have been building robot-like machines for thousands of years. Around 350 BCE, a Greek named Archytas of Tarentum created the first automaton, or machine that could move by itself. Archytas's wooden bird could fly hundreds of feet into the air.

In the early 1500s, Leonardo da Vinci created a mechanical lion that could walk.

It was not until 1961 that robots came into everyday use. That year, General Motors started using a robotic arm to

MEET ASIMO

ASIMO is a **humanoid** robot created by Honda. At 51 inches (130 cm) tall, ASIMO is just the right size to help people pick up objects or navigate stairs or sidewalks. ASIMO can turn on a light switch, push carts, and carry a tray. It can walk, run, follow commands, and even recognize faces. Someday ASIMO may do tasks such as getting snacks and turning off lights for people who are elderly or disabled. It may even help fight fires or clean up toxic spills.

Honda first introduced ASIMO in 2000.

help build cars in its factories. Today, robots are used for a wide variety of tasks, including vacuuming floors and defusing bombs. Scientists keep thinking up new kinds of robots to help us with hard, dirty, dangerous, and boring jobs.

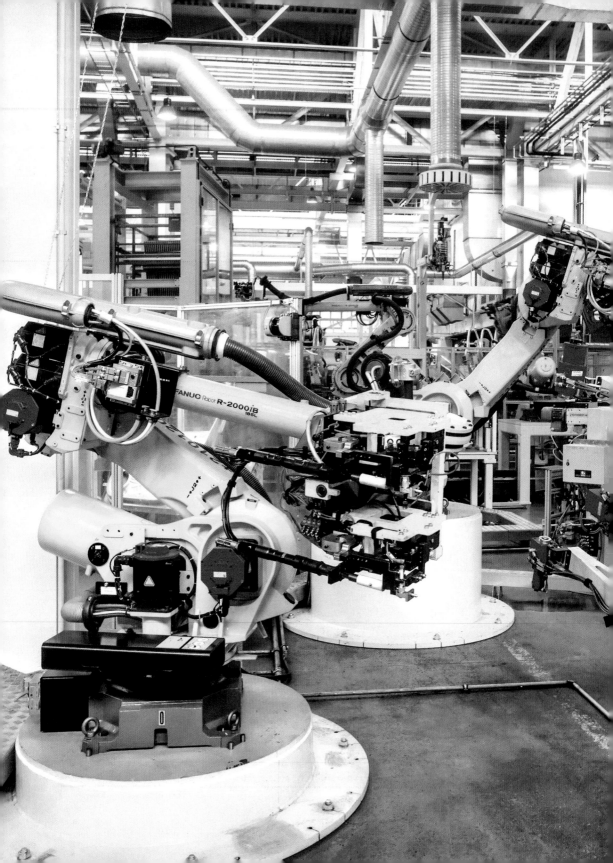

CHAPTER 2

ARE ROBOTS GOOD OR BAD?

Why do we need robots? Why not let humans do all the work? Unlike humans, robots do not get worn out when they do dull jobs. Robots can often work faster than humans and with fewer errors. They can do difficult jobs, such as lifting heavy car parts on a factory floor.

Today, car companies use many different types of robots to produce vehicles.

They can also do dirty jobs, such as checking sewage pipes for clogs.

Robots can do dangerous jobs as well. Specialized robots can climb down into a volcano to study it. They can search through rubble for survivors after an earthquake.

Robots help us in many ways. But they can also have downsides. For example, some people may lose their jobs when a factory starts using robots instead of human workers. Also, **drones** may interfere with airplane flight paths.

Some people worry that advances in technology will lead to **artificial intelligence**. Then robots could make

Bomb squads use robots so that humans do not have to handle dangerous materials.

their own decisions. These decisions might not always benefit humans. Is this really possible? No one knows for sure. Many scientists think so. Others disagree. But most scientists agree the issue should be studied carefully.

CHAPTER 3

WHAT MAKES A ROBOT TICK?

As humans, we use our senses to gather information about the world. We use our brains to process that information, and we use our muscles to act. Robots work in much the same way. They use microphones, cameras, and even heat sensors to gather information about the things around them.

Some robots are sent underwater to do jobs that are difficult or dangerous for humans.

This information then goes to the robot's "brain," or computer system, for processing. The computer system sends a message to the **actuators**. These motors may move robotic arms or turn wheels. For all of this to happen, robots also need a power source. Common power sources include batteries and solar panels.

There are many different kinds of robots. A telerobot is a remote-controlled robot that allows people to explore a place without actually being there in person. This type of robot can be used for exploration. Doctors can also use telerobots to meet with patients through a computer screen.

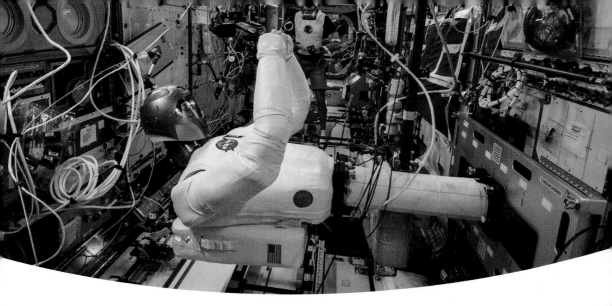

An astronaut works with Robonaut 2 to test its ability to move.

Autonomous robots do not need to be controlled by humans. A simple example is the Roomba. This small robot vacuums floors.

Androids are robots that look like humans. An android named Robonaut 2 is now being tested at the International Space Station. It may one day help astronauts with tasks.

CHAPTER 4

ROBOTS EVERYWHERE!

Most robots are in factories. They can work faster than humans. And they can work 24 hours a day without getting tired. These robots do not look like humans. Many are just a single arm.

Robots are used on farms, too. Robotic milkers free farmers from the time-consuming job of milking.

This robot can milk a cow without the farmer being there.

When a cow walks into a stall, a robotic arm reaches out and begins milking the cow. When the milk flow stops, the tubes detach and the cow leaves.

Farmers can also use robots to plant, weed, and harvest their crops. They can use drones to check if crops need water, **pesticides**, or **fertilizers**.

THE *CURIOSITY* MARS ROVER

Scientists sent the *Curiosity* rover to Mars in 2011. Since 2012, this 9.5-foot (2.9-m) robot has been testing rocks and soil. It has also sent many photographs back to Earth. The rover's mission is to find out whether life ever existed on Mars.

The *Curiosity* rover studies the climate and geology of Mars.

Robots are perfect for exploring places that are difficult or dangerous for humans to reach. For example, underwater robots can map the ocean floor.

Volcanoes are another frontier that robots are exploring. A small, two-wheeled robot called the VolcanoBot was specially built to explore cracks in volcanoes. Scientists hope the robot will help them learn more about how volcanoes erupt.

Robots are very useful for dangerous jobs. They can carry nuclear fuel to reactors. They can also carry away waste for disposal. This means humans are not exposed to **radiation**.

The ReWalk suit is a medical robot. Using this robot, people with spinal cord damage can stand, walk, and even climb stairs.

Robotic surgery is often safer than human surgery because it is more precise.

The da Vinci surgical robot is another medical robot. It has three arms that hold surgical tools. A fourth arm holds a light and camera. A doctor sits nearby. She moves controls as though she is playing a video game. The robot carries out each of the doctor's moves.

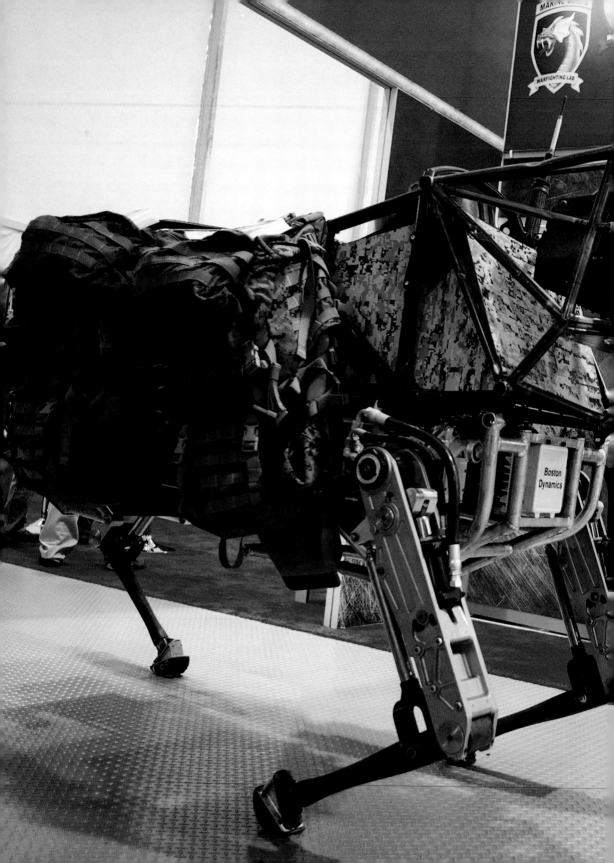

CHAPTER 5

ROBOTS OF THE FUTURE

In the future, robots will likely become even more common. Robots will plant, water, and trim crops on farms. Self-driving cars are already being tested on the road. And tiny robots may crawl through the body to deliver medicines.

Robots will do even more of the most dangerous jobs such as mining.

Military robots such as this supply-carrying robot are likely to become more common.

They will also continue to explore new frontiers. A new android astronaut called R5 may someday explore Mars, asteroids, and beyond.

Would you like to be a roboticist? If so, you will need to learn lots of science and

ROBOT SWARMS

Someday, buildings and bridges may be built by swarms of microbots. These tiny robots work together like ants. They are controlled by magnets. Scientists created a group of six microbots that is strong enough to pull a car. These MicroTugs weigh as much as a bar of soap, but they can pull nearly 2,000 times their own weight.

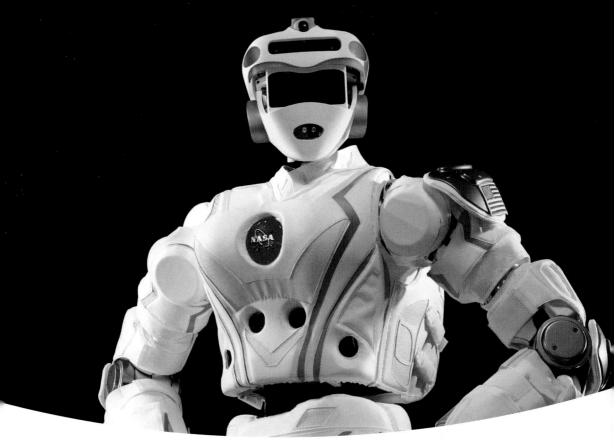

The R5 robot may someday help astronauts make repairs and gather materials.

math. But you don't have to wait until you're an adult to start designing robots.

Check your local library for books and workshops on robotics. Perhaps one day your robotic creations will explore faraway planets or dive the deepest seas!

DRIVERLESS CARS

Before long, self-driving cars will be a common sight on the highway. Google and other companies are already testing these cars in several states. Driverless cars use the global positioning system (GPS), similar to most modern cars. The GPS tells the car where it is on a map.

computer: receives information and adjusts the car's direction and speed

electronic brake: slows the car to avoid obstacles

electric battery: powers the car

Driverless cars also use dozens of sensors to gather information about their surroundings. This information is then sent to the car's computer. The computer uses the GPS and sensor information to help the car reach its destination.

sensors: lasers, radar, and cameras that sense the car's surroundings

seats: comfortable seats for passengers

FOCUS ON
ROBOTS

Write your answers on a separate piece of paper.

1. Write a letter to a friend describing what you learned about androids.

2. Would you want to ride in self-driving car? Why or why not?

3. What is one thing robots can use to gather information about the things around them?

   A. actuators
   B. solar panels
   C. heat sensors

4. What type of robot would be best for destroying cancer cells?

   A. nanobot
   B. drone
   C. android

Answer key on page 32.

GLOSSARY

actuators
Parts that put something into action, such as motors.

androids
Robots with a human appearance.

artificial intelligence
The ability of a machine to think and make decisions on its own.

autonomous
Able to move or take action without outside help.

drones
Aircraft or ships that are controlled remotely or operate on their own.

fertilizers
Substances that help plants grow.

humanoid
Shaped like or acting like a person.

nanobots
Tiny robots that are small enough to go inside the body.

pesticides
Chemicals that kill unwanted plants or animals.

radiation
Energy in the form of waves or particles.

TO LEARN MORE

BOOKS

Kortenkamp, Steve. *Future Explorers: Robots in Space*. North Mankato, MN: Capstone Press, 2016.

Mooney, Carla. *Awesome Military Robots*. Minneapolis: Abdo Publishing, 2015.

Spilsbury, Richard, and Louise Spilsbury. *Robots in Medicine*. New York: Gareth Stevens Publishing, 2016.

NOTE TO EDUCATORS

Visit **www.focusreaders.com** to find lesson plans, activities, links, and other resources related to this title.

INDEX